Jean Anouilh

by

MARGUERITE ARCHER

 **Columbia University Press**

NEW YORK & LONDON 1971

COLUMBIA ESSAYS ON MODERN WRITERS
is a series of critical studies of English,
Continental, and other writers whose works are of contemporary
artistic and intellectual significance.

Editor

William York Tindall

Advisory Editors

Jacques Barzun   W. T. H. Jackson   Joseph A. Mazzeo

Jean Anouilh is Number 55 of the series

MARGUERITE ARCHER
is an Assistant Professor in the Department of
Romance Languages at the Herbert H. Lehman College of the City
University of New York.

Jean Anouilh

In October of 1969, Jean Anouilh's twenty-ninth play, *Cher Antoine*, opened in Paris. The first-night audience was extremely enthusiastic; many clearly thought what several critics who attended the performance later wrote, that the play was a masterpiece and the author among the greatest of contemporary French playwrights. It was time for the curtain call, for the author to come forward to receive the audience's acclaim. But to the confusion of all, even the embarrassment of some, the author had left. Simply left, vanished into the Parisian night as though he had nothing to do with the play.

This refusal to acknowledge the plaudits of the audience entirely baffled the spectators. It almost seemed to some as though the playwright was trying to prolong the spell he had cast on his audience. To the public, still caught up in the death of his supposed double, the leading character, the presence of Anouilh on stage would have seemed tantamount to a resurrection.

The final scene had found the house of the now-defunct Antoine being boarded up as a handful of acquaintances recalled his admiration for the ending of Chekhov's *The Cherry Orchard*. In that play, too, a house which had once sheltered a happy family is boarded up while its soul remains in it forever. The question left unanswered was whether it was Antoine or Anouilh who had chosen such a nostalgic finale. The presence of this doubt meant that Anouilh had reached the high mark in the role of mystifier he had conceived for himself some forty years before. By playing on appearances, he had not intended to perform a dramatic unveiling of his soul but to lead the spectators up yet another rung of his ladder of pretending. Through a clever game of make-believe, which never ceases to be his first rule, he had achieved a fusion of illusion and reality in the spectators' minds. He had convinced them that, although he had formerly remained mute about private matters, he had stepped on stage that night to expose a large part of his emotional life.

Yet Anouilh was caught at his own game. The leitmotiv in *Cher Antoine* dealt with the solitude and disenchantment which overcame a playwright who, absorbed in his craft, let love pass him by. Like his grease-painted counterpart, Antoine de Saint-Flour, Anouilh felt too alienated to relieve his loneliness by accepting the acclaim of an excited crowd.

While delighting the spectators, who believed themselves to be in full command of the situation, the playwright was reveling in the ultimate theatrical trick. He had succeeded in enmeshing them in such a mixture of reality and dramatic fiction that they could not distinguish one from the other. Thus Anouilh had brilliantly resolved the essential polarity of his art and fulfilled his wish to "detheatricalize" the stage, which for him means to reduce the distance between the spectator and the stage, so that the spectator becomes an integral part of the play and does not know the difference between make-believe and reality.

Ever since he set out to make the French theatre his with *L'Hermine* in 1931, Jean Anouilh has aroused great curiosity, and sometimes ire, among critics and public alike. The controversies which arise about his plays stem from the fact that he escapes clear-cut identification. This is due not to obscurity in his *œuvre* or deviousness on his part but simply to the Protean aspect of his plays. They are variations on given themes, and as such they give the impression that they constitute contradictions. This apparent inconsistency may originate in the ambiguous behavior of the protagonists. But it is simply a fact of life that ambiguity is an integral component of man's plight in relation to himself and others; thus to ask that an image of man be in clear and unambiguous focus is to ask for comforting falsehood. Besides, if man is a "disconsolate but gay animal," as Anouilh asserts, won't he be a paradox to himself?

The isolated works of some authors give evidence of those authors' characteristics, but a particular play of Anouilh reveals at best only a few elements of his work, never his total make-up. Any one of his plays can only be judged as one hue in the spectrum of his *œuvre*. It is interesting to discover that a reading of all of Anouilh's plays reveals a yearning on the author's part to treat each piece as a step in a progression. This interpretation is supported by the presence in newer plays of lines quoted from preceding plays. And as one notes in novels of Balzac or Faulkner, mere names in earlier parts of Anouilh's work appear as full-fledged characters in later plots.

Over the years Anouilh has been recognized as one of the world's leading dramatists: his works are among the most frequently performed everywhere. Experimental theatres, repertory companies, drama schools, and avid readers constantly seek out his plays. He is best known in the United States for the success on Broadway of *The Lark* and *Becket,* and for the innumerable revivals of the irrepressible *Thieves' Carnival,* as well as *Ring Round the Moon* and *Antigone. The Lark,* Anouilh's version of Joan of Arc's martyrdom, received such acclaim that two English translations of it appeared the year it was performed. *Becket* has been transposed into a remarkable motion picture.

Throughout his long career Anouilh's fame has been quite solid. Proclaimed a young avant-gardist in the thirties, he showed great promise in competition with a constellation of stage directors such as Georges Pitoëff, Charles Dullin, André

Barsacq, Jacques Copeau, and Louis Jouvet who were steering the French stage away from realism, toward stylization, classicism, and poetry. In the forties and early fifties, the decades of the Existentialist dramatists, Anouilh continued to attract audiences with the contemporary interpretation of a Greek theme in *Antigone* and the dramatization of man's sense of dedication in *Becket*. In 1959 he boldly endorsed the brash anti-plays of Ionesco, Adamov, and Samuel Beckett. He went so far as to urge his public to go down the street from the theatre where one of his plays was being performed to see Ionesco's *Les Chaises,* and he unreservedly praised *Waiting for Godot* when Samuel Beckett was virtually unknown. Strangely enough, the birth of the anti-theatre may well be the reason for a six-year silence on his part. At any rate, he created nothing of his own between *L'Orchestre* (1962) and *Le boulanger, la boulangère et le petit mitron* (1969), the success of which placed him again in the forefront of contemporary drama. Six years meant a long silence for a man who in thirty-eight years has published thirty plays, has adapted works varying from Shakespeare to Oscar Wilde, who has created scenarios, made records, written newspaper articles, and even produced a book of scathing fables. But between October, 1969, and February, 1970, Anouilh presented two plays, *Cher Antoine* and *Les Poissons rouges,* which provoked wild raves and renewed his love affair with his public. Thus time has shown that "The Great Anouilh," as he is called in France, who once said that a playwright is a gentleman who seduces a lady, she being the public, can lay claim to the place of Don Juan in the field of drama.

Jean Anouilh, now a distinguished French gentleman with beautiful blue eyes and a serene expression, was born on June 23, 1910, in the rich Atlantic port of Bordeaux. His father was a tailor noted for the scrupulousness with which he exercised his skills. Stage directors who feel too restricted by Anouilh's minute descriptions of his characters' stances bemoan the fact that he inherited this particular trait. His mother, a violinist, often played with the orchestra of the casino of Arcachon, a quaint seaside resort forty-five minutes from Bordeaux on the adorably lackadaisical shuttle train. It was in Arcachon that his fascination for theatrics was nurtured, for as a little boy he had the privilege of gazing, baffled, at the operettas performed night after night for vacationers. If the actors were second-rate, they nevertheless mesmerized his imagination through their magic ability to play specific, well-defined roles. Since then, orchestra members and struggling actors have kept a unique place in his heart, appearing with various traits in *L'Hermine, Eurydice, La Sauvage, Le Rendez-vous de Senlis*. When one sees Anouilh in the Bordeaux region, one can still detect in his demeanor a sort of pantheistic pleasure. Although he refrains from displaying his exhilaration, he affectionately calls this area the birthplace of good humanists. Among them he counts Montaigne, with whom he joins in pleading for reason and moderation on the part of men.

When he was nine, he moved to Paris with his parents and lived in the Montmartre district, where some of his plays would be shown later on. At the age of thirteen he precociously wrote in verse what he calls "false plays" which he acted out for friends and relatives. After elementary schooling at the Ecole Colbert, he pursued traditional studies at the Collège Chaptal. Jean-Louis Barrault, a classmate, recalled him as a distant, nattily attired young man, difficult to get to know. Thirty years later, in 1959, the two were to create *La petite Molière*, starring Anouilh's daughter Catherine. Going to law school after he finished at Chaptal must have seemed drab to the aspiring dramatist, especially after a balmy spring evening in 1928 when he was irremediably captivated by Giraudoux's *Siegfried*. (It is from Giraudoux, Anouilh confesses, that he learned the sense of stylization which characterizes all his theatre.) Soon after, he created *Mandarine* (1929). *Humulus le muet*, which has yet to be performed, was written the same year in collaboration with Jean Aurenche, whom Anouilh met when he repudiated law and started working in an advertising agency. The same pair co-authored four film scenarios between 1936 and 1939. About his training in publicity Anouilh confides that, in lieu of poetic studies, slogans taught him the precision and timing essential to dialogue. In 1930, while awaiting the call to military service, he became Louis Jouvet's secretary-general at the Comédie des Champs-Elysées, where most of his plays are performed today. Receiving in effect no guidance from the famous actor-director largely responsible for the success of the *Siegfried* he so idolized, Anouilh found the position disappointing and lonely. Still undaunted, he wrote *L'Hermine*, which was presented at the Théâtre de l'Oeuvre by Pierre Fresnay in 1932. Acclaimed as a promising young dramatist, Anouilh resolved to dedicate his life to the theatre. When in 1935 he sold to Metro-Goldwyn-Mayer the rights to *Y'avait un prisonnier*, he gained the financial independence that enabled him to start devoting his life to writing.

Although his work seems effortless at times, it betrays the unquenched thirst for growth and renewal of a playwright acutely engaged in the present, a man of letters who would hate to admit that he never forgot the classicist Boileau's admonition to polish and repolish one's creations. His desire for constant improvement is illustrated by the various collections of his plays.

Anouilh has said that his grouping of plays under the headings of *pièces noires, nouvelles pièces noires, pièces roses, pièces brillantes, pièces grinçantes,* and *pièces costumées* (that is: black plays, new black plays, rosy plays, polished plays, grating plays, and costume plays) aims to satisfy the public's need for classifications. As he indicates, we must consider such divisions somewhat arbitrary, since he did not write all the plays included in a collection at one time. But the groups nevertheless represent the different phases of his evolution.

Pièces noires (black plays) are not tragedies in the classical sense of the word but dramas in the sense that they display the defeat of individuals in their quest to live within the framework of society and humanity, while at the same time preserving the self. The term "tragedy" would seem overly formal to the unpretentious Anouilh, who at the onset of his vocation aspired to nothing more than the role of a man of the theatre in the image of Molière, the writer capable of distracting men from their cares. The volume of *pièces noires* includes *L'Hermine* (1931), *La Sauvage* (1934), *Le Voyageur sans bagage* (1936), and *Eurydice* (1941). These names evoke a gallery of portraits, as Anouilh intends essentially to act as portraitist. Each painting represents the stylization of an individual, with his past, his present dilemma, his own interior climate. But while *L'Hermine*, *La Sauvage*, and *Le Voyageur sans bagage* take place in a post-World War I setting, *Eurydice* moves in the timelessness of myth. Because the characters all have the same choice to make, they may be put into identical frameworks. In order to find serenity, each must decide whether to reject or acquiesce in his destiny, as it is assigned to him either by society or by more obscure forces.

Consider *L'Hermine* (English translation, *The Ermine*). In a society dominated by the bourgeoisie, Frantz, a young man without money, loves the rich Monime. Her aunt opposes their marriage and a prosperous man thwarts Frantz's attempt to acquire the sum he needs. The young man must renounce Monime, or marry her and condemn her to a shameful life of lowly prospects. Convinced that old women serve no purpose, he kills the rich aunt in order to use her money "to build an indestructible barrier around his love." Blind with

[9]

rancor at seeing men's rules bar the way to his will to be happy, he defies those rules and stands alone as the monster-martyr born from the monetary shackles invented by man. He can survive only if he rejects the society which threatened to deprive him of the right to acquire happiness. His situation recalls Rousseau's image of man as being enslaved by the advent of the merciless social organization men have plotted.

Anouilh creates Thérèse, the main character of *La Sauvage* (English translation, *Restless Heart*) from his memories of the second-rate musicians who used to play in European cafés in the thirties. His sympathy for these somewhat grotesque figures grew from an understanding of the tragedy inherent in their lives. They provided him with many a character for the *pièces noires,* since the gap between the life they led and the one to which they aspired was so deep. They lived under the illusion that with their talent they deserved applause and the finer things of life, but in reality they received less and less of both each day. For Anouilh, they symbolized in a stylized manner the fate of the common man, trying to find permanence in a world reduced to shambles by the financial Depression of the early thirties, a world moving inexorably toward World War II.

Thérèse is young, like all the principal characters in the *pièces noires,* and she represents the reexamination of accepted values to which the young proceed throughout history. Born to shabby musicians who are on the watch for the stroke of luck which will change their fate, she rejects her love for Florent, a talented pianist with whom life would mean wealth and happiness. Her obstinate efforts to show him the sordid-ness of her background, so as to repel him, appear masochistic. In Anouilh's terms, however, she accepts her true condition, which is one of suffering, deeming her action more worthy of a human being than giving in to happiness, which for her would be the same as accepting to live a lie.

Gaston, in *Le Voyageur sans bagage* (English translation, *Traveller without Luggage*), betrays a yearning for the innocence of a child. He seeks the "Noble Savage" in himself. As a former amnesiac looking for his past, he is distressed to discover that his family created a cruel jungle instead of a home, and worse yet, that he too behaved in a despicable manner. Destiny provides him with an escape from his family, but he has to kill his past, even in this escape, and killing anything is sad. Here the play intimates that a man must cut his ties with other human beings in order to acquire the freshness of spirit and nobility of character he desires.

The heroine in *Eurydice* moves within the pitiful circle of second-rate actors, attached to a mother for whom life is the series of clichés she has heard in bad plays. Like all the young heroines in Anouilh's theatre, she emerges out of the playwright's boyish love affair with the ingénues he saw at Arcachon. Although his instinct taught him that they were marked by many male hands, he has etched them throughout his work as abused but innocent females of the species whose hearts remain as pure as Iphigenia's. They receive nicknames such as "The Wild One" (La Sauvage), "The Dove" (Colombe), "The Lark" (l'Alouette). With their strong libidos hidden by a rough beauty which nothing mars, they remain his porcelain dolls.

Eurydice's past takes the physical aspect of men's fingerprints left all over her body. She no longer remembers how they came to be there, but Orpheus sees them as so many disgusting tattoos. He knows they are part of her experience of life. When she might slip confidently into the euphoria of love, and pictures her future relationship with Orpheus, she remembers that because of her past she lacks the virginity of soul she wishes she could offer to Orpheus. Unable to remove the marks, she chooses to die and thus redeem herself. Even Orpheus cannot save her, for when she is given a chance to return to life, he unwittingly lets her die again by indulging in his own jealousy. Eventually, he too choses death, which seems to be the only realm where one may find gentle peace, beauty, pure love, and the cleansing of one's soul.

As we look at these plays as a whole, it is clear that the same yearning for complete freedom and integrity drives all the protagonists to despair, although the circumstances vary. In Anouilh's vision, every sight, every touch, every experience, every moment of time, leave their imprint on man's soul and preclude any rebirth of interior freshness, of innocence. Man seems to resemble a sheet of blotting paper which can never be cleansed of its spots, even though he wishes to regain his purity.

In addition, according to their heredity, their past history of poverty or wealth, pain or pleasure, men are divided into two races which cannot communicate: as Baudelaire expressed it, the race of Cain and the race of Abel. When the protagonists could be saved by redeemerlike characters who would graciously give of themselves to prevent their beloved's fate, they respond with a sardonic but melancholy refusal. For example, when Florent pleads with Thérèse to take his love and the serenity he promises, she refuses, and as he stands bewildered, she tells him that he must accept the role of a stranger on earth, the role of a king who possesses all, without having suffered for it. Florent feels unjustly accused of some sort of crime, while Thérèse implies that she will remain in a brotherhood of men based on their destitution. Neither of the two seems to have a real freedom of choice. Yet they must find a bearable stance in a world which holds them accountable for what is actually imposed on them by pure chaos.

As he developed the cycle of the *pièces noires*, Anouilh was accused of treating only one subject. Actually, these four plays constitute variations on the dilemma of life. As such, they tend to show the pride, the yearnings, the frustrations of certain characters rather than to expose the definitive philosophy of the dramatist. At this point in his career the young playwright was primarily concerned with the creation of characters, not with the growth of plot, hence the enigmatic quality of the characters' rejection. From the debates the characters engage in, however, general trends of thought can be deduced, which Anouilh elaborates more fully in later plays. What mainly stands out in his early work is an interest in the complexity of man's motives and the difficulties of making a lucid choice in the chaotic modern world which pulls a man in opposite directions.

Many interpretations of Anouilh's use of the money theme have been developed. Actually, his basic design, which is that of a moralist studying men's visible responses to social stimulants, is similar to that in works of fiction showing men adjusting to love, family, politics, and money. He explains that he observes men from the "moral" point of view, which to him means dealing with a choice of behavior that either does or does not conform to accepted standards, not only of ethics, but also of custom and taste. He does not aim to create purely psychological or metaphysical plays, but attempts to hold a mirror up to his fellow men. However, even though he is not conscious of the fact, his astute studies of their conduct slip into meditations on man's psyche and on the human condition, especially in the serious plays. For instance, the murder perpetrated by Frantz in *L'Hermine* changes into a symbolic triumph over frustration. The old aunt, who personifies money, becomes the scapegoat of Frantz's anxiety. He is afraid of his possible inability to love forever, of his desires, of his vulnerability. The girl he loves has the purity of a lily. To deserve her, he dreams of possessing a crystal-clear soul, cleansed of all the blemishes living as a poor man has left.

Once the case of each hero in the *pièces noires* is examined, one realizes that the premise given at the very beginning of the play, involving only the way in which he will find serenity or happiness, becomes the academic question: Does the order of life, the make-up of man, the nature of the world, allow any man to achieve happiness or peace within himself? In Anouilh's kaleidoscope, at this point, the answer is negative. For life transforms and erodes the subject and the object of happiness to different degrees; it may be impossible for man to subscribe to serenity within himself, although he keeps thinking that he desires it above all things; at the same time, society nullifies man's effort toward his own fulfillment by enslaving him with mass-produced rules. In *Antigone,* Anouilh will go so far as to advance the theory that happiness is only a human fabrication.

These dramas appeal by the fact that they enrich us with unconventional images of young individuals in search of a *modus vivendi.* The characters cannot be placed in neatly labeled boxes, for they fit into no system, except the one created by their own identities and Anouilh's stylization. As he makes them define themselves in lucid, realistic dialogue ranging from the virulent to the pathetic, he puts us in the presence of individuals who manage to remain unforgettable. From their original expression of universal misery emanates a certain poetry associated with our vision of the young romantic making his stand in a harsh, absurd world. Finally, it is interesting to see how, while portraying the painful awakening of youth to the inequities brought by life lived among other men, Anouilh casually slips into philosophical metaphors, refreshingly stripped of authoritarian pronouncements.

The *nouvelles pièces noires* (new black plays) encompass *Jézabel* (1932), *Antigone* (1942), *Roméo et Jeannette* (1945), and *Médée* (1946). It is logical that Anouilh, who stayed away from realism in his early plays, would turn to myth for the creation of two of these plays, *Antigone* and *Médée*, for myth approaches poetry in its moving display of the human condition. He was attracted by myth on several grounds. First, the successful modernization of myths accomplished by Giraudoux and Cocteau proved justifiably inspiring. Second, the themes sung in myths fitted in with Anouilh's penchant for examining man's struggle to escape from social, psychological, or metaphysical bondage. Finally, the rejuvenation of mythical characters posed a challenge to Anouilh's capacity for developing the personalities of his protagonists, a development which must be carefully done if re-creation of myth is to be valid.

Although not literally mythical, *Jézabel* and *Roméo et Jeannette* fit into the collection of the *nouvelles pièces noires* because the fate of their title characters is as well known as that of Antigone and Medea: they are an integral and unforgettable part of man's literary history. The fact that the shadow of death grows inexorably larger with each swing of the pendulum, while the spectator watches helplessly the hero or heroine being engulfed, gives these plays an atmosphere of tragedy. And the stylistic restraint in *Antigone*, *Roméo et Jeannette*, and *Médée* contributes to the timeless classical quality of their development and resolution.

As the generic title indicates, the *nouvelles pièces noires* stand closely linked to the *pièces noires;* all the plays together form a progression, with each gaining a larger degree of impact. In *L'Hermine*, *La Sauvage*, and *Le Voyageur sans bagage*, the prime origin of fate rests in the inflexibility of the characters, in their polarization. Though they represent extremes, they do deserve understanding, even sympathy, for we share a thin affinity with them. Jézabel's fate arises from weakness, it awakens fear that we, like her, may succumb to our own flaws; hence identification grows stronger. The fate of Frédéric and Jeannette is born from imponderables. We pity these lovers who mysteriously disintegrate as if eaten by a baffling disease of the mind. In the case of Antigone and Médée, destiny depends on the whims of the gods, regardless of the characters' own innocence or guilt. Their situation takes on awesome proportions, for it arbitrarily withdraws from the individual the chance to save himself through any sort of asceticism, no matter how hard the attempt may be. So we wonder whether our freedom, like theirs, is illusory, for we know that we struggle too and don't always succeed; complete empathy follows. In Anouilh's view, our emotional reaction means that he has accomplished the feat of reverting the theatre back to its essence, which is communion: he has succeeded in shocking the public out of its cruelly callous attitude toward its fellow beings. We see that, as he has patiently humanized his characters to a greater extent with each play, the intensity of the impact on the audience has increased. All the while he continues to exploit the same general pattern of themes. Each play mixes the elements of choice and alienation: each plot develops within the narrow social confines of a couple or a family, except *Antigone,* which widens to include the political circle. Generally (*Jézabel* being the exception), the *nouvelles pièces noires* offer an ennobling picture of man's courage.

Jézabel, a disturbing play, opens this collection, opposing its darkly grotesque atmosphere to the sublime beauty of the rest of the plays. As the title forecasts, the Jézabel of Anouilh, a counterpart of the one who slew the Lord's prophets, must indeed be eaten by the dogs, as the aging woman who poisons her husband to get his money and give it to her lover. Her son, Marc, is in love with a rich young lady from a good family. After he begs his mother to accept the fact of her age and bring decency to the family so that he may marry Jacqueline, the play assumes naturalistic overtones. Jézabel displays her drinking, her sexual urges, her slovenly appearance, in vulgar terms. Despite criticism aimed at the facile appearance of this naturalism, Anouilh later defended the validity of its use. On the occasion of his adaptation of Vitrac's *Victor,* in 1962, he said that naturalism is actually "not a photograph of reality, but a careful reproduction of that accepted notion of life which has become life itself"; in other words, it is the stylization of an already stylized reproduction of life, therefore not the result of facility. In truth, *Jézabel,* despite its unevenness, goes far beyond its naturalistic level and deserves a reappraisal. Its central character, in all her pitiful abhorrence, reflects many a real human being in the courts, prisons, drug addict rehabilitation centers. Her condition provokes long meditations about the fall of humanity. Unlike Antigone or Medea, Jézabel lacks a personal identity and searches for it in men's arms, only to find herself completely bewildered by their semi-animalistic responses. She rejects life in the sense that she cannot accept what it has done to her husband, now a man deprived of all enthusiasm. She recalls Eurydice and Antigone when she seems to say that death is indeed preferable to old age and the day-to-day deprivations entailed by the passing of time.

Written in 1932, this play has the obsessive quality and the impact of Sartre's *No Exit;* Jézabel and her son become each other's hell; he is her hell because no matter how she explains her sordidness, he judges her on his own terms; she is his hell because he knows he is like her and he tries desperately to change her image so he can be saved.

Besides its philosophical implications, *Jézabel* offers a somber comment on motherhood. It becomes a farce in which a woman requires a commitment from her husband and children on the ground that she is a mother, but then concerns herself solely with her beauty creams, her obsession with youth, and her lovers. The husband, in this burlesque ballet, invariably retreats to the status of a nonentity, allowing himself to be overwhelmed by his wife's selfish recriminations. Instead of acting as the revered legendary head of the family, he turns out to be a beggar who hangs onto his children's coattails for sympathy and even financial support.

In *Antigone*, as the Chorus remarks, we should enjoy a measure of serenity. We are told that we are among equals, for "we all are innocent." Our roles are interchangeable; one day we play the victim, another, the spectator. When the Prologue takes us into the author's confidence by introducing the actors and explaining the casting, we feel like actors ourselves, taking a busman's holiday for the evening. As we settle back calmly into our seats to observe the unraveling of the action, we are quickly snapped out of our complacency by the reminder that we are so tranquil only because tonight is not our turn to die. We are forced into the awareness that our death is but a question of time, and the play becomes not an individual story but a universal one. In this manner Anouilh, who states in *La Grotte* that the public makes the play and hence should be made to rehearse with the actors, legitimizes the presence of the Prologue in his modernization of the myth by using it directly to manipulate his spectator. Thus he provides the audience with the necessary distance to bear the sorrows they will witness and, at the same time, the closeness which will enable them to share in the catharsis.

Antigone, the masterpiece which brought international fame to Anouilh when it was first published has only recently received the praise it deserves in the United States from the experimental theatres. Written in 1942, and performed in 1944 during the Nazi occupation of France, it aroused the most heated controversy by its double aspect of myth and political satire, for Antigone clearly symbolizes the Resistance, whereas Créon's motives were interpreted by some as an approval of the Vichy government, and by others as a veiled satire of it. As an artist, Anouilh did not have to choose sides. He meant to awaken people's consciousness to the concept of revolt. Were Créon's motives weaker than Antigone's, the play would become a clear-cut case of the triumph of good over evil, which would satisfy the emotions but not the intellect, for it would provide too simplistic a view of man's dilemmas.

At the time, it was particularly daring of Anouilh to modernize a myth sustained by a political conflict. The French suffered daily from increasing restrictions which seemed the more arbitrary since they were dictated to the Vichy government by the Nazis. The nation was divided into a camp advocating revolt and a camp accepting the Occupation as inevitable. By giving the tragedy an enigmatic meaning which does not exist in the Sophocles play, Anouilh was offering the partisans in the Resistance the delight of interpreting Antigone's gesture as one of support for them, while the Nazis were unable to censure the play since Créon made such a good case for civic obedience. Nevertheless, the presence of this doubt resulted in strong abuse of Anouilh by those who misinterpreted his purpose. It was in *Pauvre Bitos*, published after the Liberation, that the playwright squelched those excessive and unfounded attacks.

Antigone, a skinny girl whom no one takes seriously, decides to challenge the so-called order of the world, knowing full well that she will be condemned to die for her boldness. In this she resembles her Greek counterpart, but, unlike the classical Antigone, this young girl shows far more vulnerability and hardly conveys the notion that she is a heroic figure. After she attempts to bury Polynice, she runs promptly to her Nurse's arms for human warmth and security; she admits on several occasions that she is afraid; and while waiting to be entombed, she asks the guard what it is like to die.

As she becomes increasingly shaken by Créon's arguments, she expresses her motives less and less clearly. Whereas she starts by asserting that she has to bury her brother out of fraternal love, she ends up by sighing that she does not know any more why she has chosen to die. This baffling response confers a seemingly insoluble ambiguity to the play. But the very evolution of her moral purpose eventually explains the mystery and removes some of its enigma.

As she talks to her sister Ismène at the onset of the action, Antigone appears to be a melancholy instrument of fate, regretting her role, saying that Créon's part is to decide her death, while hers is to bury her brother and accept that death as the consequence. Her action at this stage takes on the value of a clearly defined duty. Her disobedience stems from a fatal necessity dictated by the customs which advocate that the Dead must be symbolically laid to rest by the Living to escape the penalty of wandering forever in pain over the face of the earth.

When Ismène pleads for an "understanding" of the complexity of the situation and tries to explain the impossibility of making the right choice and the frightful consequences of disobedience, Antigone's anger flares up. The concept of "understanding" strikes her as a cowardly escape from responsibility, as fear of unrestrained life. If she chooses to die, does it mean that she does not feel like living? asks Ismène. Antigone answers by nostalgically reviewing her awareness of the validity of life. She recalls the contemplation of a garden in the solitude of daybreak, the sense of wonder one has at the sight of millions of insects endowed with life, running through an incalculable number of living blades of grass. Later on she indicates that living could also gain meaning through her love for Hémon, through procreation out of that love, through the relationship shared by members of a family. It becomes clear then that so complete is her knowledge of the value of life that the prospect of suffering or dying does not constitute enough of a deterrent to prevent her from living independently of any restriction, if only once, and even if the penalty for it be annihilation. At that point, her original moral purpose is reinforced by her need to live in the absolute sense of the word, to commit herself completely to living.

Her crucial confrontation with Créon takes her a step further. As he accuses her of being guilty of extreme pride, of making a display of personal pathos, of following in Oedipus' footsteps, of engaging in a contest with Destiny and Death, in a word, of showing "hubris," he strengthens her decision to do "what she can" regardless of the consequences, as a simple human being, not as a king's daughter, and because it is her duty to do so. At the beginning she was going to bury her brother because it was expected of her; now she wills it, as the one act which is in her power to perform, the act which gives her an identity.

When Créon describes the funeral rites as a sham, a series of pharisaic gestures that even she should be ashamed of, Antigone is submerged by a sudden awareness of the absurdity of customs. She resents the hodgepodge of fallacious constraints and the artificial, senseless, and arbitrary nature of any limitation which man allows to impede his right to live as he wants. She visualizes a complete revenge on this absurdity. Her act will be carried out in total freedom, as she desires. In the face of arbitrariness, there does not have to be any necessity to her act other than that which she imposes on it. She sarcastically tells Créon that she will accomplish her mission "for herself." In so doing, she will commit an absurdity to limit the absurdity which limitations impose upon man; customs, rules, the state, the human condition will hem in life only so far as it wants to be hemmed in; she transcends the human condition, just as she decides to transcend pain when Créon twists her arm and she blurts out that it does not hurt, since for all intents and purposes she has no arm. Inasmuch as she chooses to impose her own rules and meaning on what happens to her, she can scorn Créon and declare that it is she who has become the Queen, while he has become the slave of events. Antigone's solution is to impose her own absurdity on the universal absurdity, as a means of conquering it.

Her moment of glory is temporarily reversed, however, when Créon discloses the sordidness of both brothers' characters and the consequent meaninglessness of his choice to bury one and desecrate the other. After this blow Antigone considers repudiating her decision; in a daze, she mumbles "yes" when Créon tells her to go home and marry Hémon. But as the knot of the action tightens and Créon, on the threshold of victory, equates life and happiness, Antigone's moral purpose crystallizes in a flash. Men use "filthy happiness" to cover up their hypocrisy. Happiness serves to mask the lies, the compromises, the calculations which men cowardly accept so that they may go on living, so that they may avoid danger and death. Happiness is a masquerade of life itself and she will not settle for living on those terms. She wants a full life even if it holds no hope of lasting. Therefore, she subscribes completely to her fate, proud to carry out the pursuit of truth begun by her father, Oedipus.

Still Antigone becomes distraught despite her resolve. The world has turned into a void. As she dictates a letter to Hémon just before her death, she sighs that she does not know any more why she dies. And neither do we. Her choice started out as a moral necessity, changed into the rejection of the human condition, then to an endorsement of absurdity, and finally disintegrates into nothingness. In the end, she is committing a totally gratuitous act, thereby illustrating the inexplicability of our actions. To the Chorus who begs him not to let Antigone die, Créon answers that Polynice was a pretext for her and that, when she renounced her first premise, she found another, for what mattered was that she die. It appears that what actually mattered was that she act.

The Chorus concludes the play with a low-keyed sort of

wail over the scheme of humanity that augments our bewilderment. It chants that men get caught and die in the struggle of opposite beliefs, whether they themselves have strong beliefs or not. Once dead, their names are soon forgotten by the living. Occasionally, one person creates havoc in the consciousness of some of his fellow men. They forgive him for it, as sad lethargy overtakes them. As to the rest of men, they continue to play cards, oblivious to it all, suggesting that an act like Antigone's cannot change the machinelike indifference of life.

So this play ends with a disturbing lack of hope for the discovery of a rational meaning to our constant strife; yet it consoles us through its existence as a moving work of art. A brilliant handling of dramatic elements gives it a satisfying homogeneity which never falls into dullness. The character development and the organization of the plot impart complete plausibility to the action. The play maintains a smooth dynamic rhythm, thanks to the perfect balance of moods. The moments of intense emotion and those of banter or trivial discussion fit carefully together with the help of the classical restraint of the language. Whereas Sophocles' play is forbidding, Anouilh's work touches the whimsical at times, allowing the modern spectator necessary respite from its strong emotional content. In the scenes involving the Nurse and the guards, the playwright not only aims at the comic relief often encountered in Shakespeare but satirizes contemporary society by introducing the notions of pieces of toast and pensions. Anouilh is irrepressible at heart, and he admits he plays such tricks to amuse himself.

He remains a master of dialogue by skillfully mixing humor with the poetic lines of Antigone as she evokes her childhood, her love for Hémon, her awe at disturbing the peace of the road in the morning light. As a result of these intricate combinations, Anouilh presents a very human though heroic Antigone who elicits curiosity, fear, pity, compassion, amusement, sorrow, and reflection; she provokes not only admiration but attachment, as if she were a real person.

Continuing his voyage through man's tragic history, Anouilh turned next to the theme of the doomed lovers. To create *Roméo et Jeannette*, he grafted that theme onto the stifling situation displayed in the *pièces noires*. The plot does not appear very logical, for Frédéric's and Jeannette's character makes them unlikely lovers. But the plausibility of their love resides in its quality. Love befalls the two, as it befell Tristan and Isolde after they drank the love philter; when it has cast its spell, the lovers resemble two prisoners trapped in the same cage, desperately trying to understand why they are enslaved; at the same time they treasure gloomily what ties them, even in the face of a presentiment that it will cause their death.

This play offers a good occasion to examine Anouilh's ideas on love. He has yet to present love as a salutary tie between man and woman; it can be sublime for a while and then it leads to death; sometimes it appears to be a grotesque masquerade among caricatures, at other times it is what people talk about in make-believe, a kind of fairy tale resembling the *pièces roses;* in *Cher Antoine*, Anouilh presents it as a miracle, blessing very few chosen people; as Lucien, Jeannette's brother warns, a promising love must be craftily hidden from "that one up there," who is jealous and will coldly steal it away. In other words, what man views as one of his few consolations on earth may be merely a myth.

The death of Frédéric and Jeannette in a purifying sea does not come as a surprise, the heroine needing redemption for the sins of carnal knowledge as much as did Eurydice. The play, meant by its title to remind us of *Romeo and Juliet*, recalls more *Tristan and Isolde*, or better still *Pelléas et Mélisande*, simply because its rhythm plunges the spectator into the sort of mystic wasteland one finds in the Maeterlinck play. Inasmuch as the central characters keep groping for a way to express their predicament, they seem far removed from Romeo and Juliet, who can elucidate so well their situation.

While the style in *Antigone* showed the firmness befitting a grandiose subject, *Roméo et Jeannette* reveals a controlled poetic fluidity which testifies to Anouilh's amazing versatility. He has explained that he first visualizes a play before he captures it on paper. This play has been transposed with its aura of unreality, as *Léocadia* will be. It offers the charms of an elegy, for the dialogue possesses a contemplative tone that puts one in a mood of gentle mourning.

Euripides emphasized a woman's potential for evil in his *Medea;* in *Médée,* Anouilh has tied the Medea myth to his microcosm, by making of it a confrontation of absolute love and life. As long as man and woman remain—according to Anouilh's favorite metaphor—two little soldiers fighting the battle of life side by side, love can last. Once the scheme of life transforms the woman into a female unaware of the man's need to merge into the stream of life and compete with other men, he reverts to being a male, and the love act becomes a somber struggle in which each partner tries to subjugate the other. Médée does not escape Anouilh's rule of life; she is transformed by her blind passion and refuses to accept any limitations to her powers. Jason has also changed; he pleads for compromises with love, with life, with men, with the world. He is ready to find a purpose in the human condition such as other men have done and to acquiesce in the form they have given the world around them. Quite often in Anouilh's work the characters who revolt against the inescapable barriers to their freedom and seem to think that courage lies in accepting death are enjoined to choose to live. For living takes a great deal of courage too, says the author, the courage of the stoic, since every day brings new suffering. Jason knows this; however, he wants to go on living, to become a man who takes pride in being himself in his totality, not with complacency but with the recognition of his potential for humble acts as well as noble ones. Médée adheres to the identity of proud outcast she chose when she betrayed father, brother, and country to favor absolute love; she demands total commitment to her absolute on Jason's part. At that point love is no longer possible between them; Médée can only choose death. She also needs to take revenge on a world which she rejects, so she kills her children. Yet we cannot help but feel pity for her, for she is a victim of fate.

The play marks an important step in Anouilh's development: for the first time in his *œuvre*, the author paints in Jason a character who, having first rejected men's rules for the sake of an absolute, comes to terms with the imperfections inherent in man's condition.

Although it is a striking play because of the solidity of its dialogue and structure, *Médée* has not yet been performed. Roland Piétri, Anouilh's co-stage director, declares that it was "killed by the public before it was performed." Anouilh himself recalls that, ever since antiquity, such has been the fate of plays involving Medea. This rejection has made him ponder once more the mysterious ways of men.

To feel a moment of joy, the spectator of the *pièces roses* is invited to join Anouilh in unadulterated fantasy. In order to create vehicles for amusement, Anouilh delves into all the resources of his imagination as well as into his experience as a stage director, for the complicated physical activity in these plays necessitates a great deal of organization. In his comedies, Anouilh resembles a cross between Molière choreographing ballet-comedies, and Feydeau compounding *quid pro quos*. For, like Molière when he had to provide entertainment for

Louis XIV's court, Anouilh makes of his comedy a spectacle, and like Feydeau, he bases the laughter on multiple plots.

In one play, *Humulus le muet* (1929; Humulus the Mute), he turns the tragic impediments of a mute young man and a deaf young girl into a hilariously funny skit.

In another, *Le Bal des voleurs* (1932; English translation, *Thieves' Carnival*), he enchants by showing the improbable gymnastics performed by thieves who try to hide their tricks from their benevolent victims. The antics executed by the characters have reminded many a critic of the spontaneity of the *commedia dell'arte*, although the apparent pell-mell of the action has been minutely timed by Anouilh. Had the play first been staged on this side of the Atlantic, *Le Bal des voleurs* might well have evolved as a comedy in the manner of the Keystone cops. Anouilh, however, transforms his thieves into characters who move across the stage with the grace of ballet dancers. In this entertainment we meet again the familiar figure of the duchess, in this case Lady Hurf. Unlike her counterpart in *L'Hermine*, however, she no longer represents the agent of ill fate, the obstacle to fulfillment; instead, continuing the generous work started by the Duchesse Dupont-Dufort in *Le Voyageur sans bagage*, she conducts herself as a benefactor bringing together the elements of happiness.

Lady Hurf, realizing that she has never really lived, amuses herself by assisting the thieves who intend to rob her. Though she penetrates their disguise as Spanish dukes, she pretends to recognize them as the real dukes. Everyone moves around her like an amiable puppet, for she is the only character who seems to exist in a concrete way; since she is the real culprit of the situation, the action centers on her and she has to explain more forcefully than the other characters her system of values.

The action reveals Anouilh at his best as a showman manipulating the strings of his creations. As to the comedy, it goes far beyond slapstick to elaborate a sort of intricate dance of pixylike but bungling thieves who at times steal from each other.

The tongue-in-cheek make-believe of *Le Bal des voleurs* bears no hint of the desperation which characterized the *pièces noires*. Gone is the need for the poor young man to commit a crime in order to deserve the rich girl he loves. The ludicrous Lord Edgar provides the hopeful suitor of the tale with the proper status by recognizing him as his once-stolen son. Quite a *deus ex machina!* In the *pièces roses*, Anouilh seems to say that all is well that ends well. If man wants to be happy, he must accept all the rules of illusion; the best formula for survival may be to choose the rosiness of illusion, instead of the blackness of reality.

Léocadia (1939; English translation, *Time Remembered*), a *Sleeping Beauty* for grown-ups, is a glorious exercise in fantasy. In this fairy tale, it is the girl, a little milliner drawn in the image of Thérèse, who brings the rich prince to life and love, after he has lost interest in both because of the death of his beloved diva. Though the theme is uncomplicated, the love story captivates, thanks to Anouilh's undeniable gift for characterization and plot construction. The happy ending of the story arises from the complementary attributes of the characters; with good-natured eccentricity the giddy duchess, hoping to create the atmosphere for love, reconstructs on her estate the setting of the prince's memories; at the same time, the tenderness and good will of the girl interact perfectly with the ethereal romanticism of the prince.

As one considers the surrealistic décor which reproduces the park where Prince Troubiscoi had met the diva, one realizes how much of the freshness of the child remains in Anouilh. The juxtaposition of the ice-cream booth, the sleepy inn awakened by the sound of violins, the legs hanging out of an old ivy-covered taxi now inhabited by rabbits, seems to jumble together a series of adolescent dreams. One can understand why Anouilh's favorite characters remain Antigone, Eurydice, Thérèse, heroines possessing the qualities of children, marching to danger like child crusaders fiercely fighting the evil powers which threaten to tarnish their innocence.

In *Léocadia*, as in all the *pièces roses*, Anouilh pleads with men to abandon their futile harshness: he shows them how easy it is to have fun and how, with a little "laissez faire," the world becomes a tenable place in which to live.

During the early part of his career, Anouilh alternated between writing *pièces noires* and *pièces roses*. Then, after effecting a kind of personal catharsis through the creation of three *nouvelles pièces noires* in a row, he immersed himself in art for art's sake with the *pièces brillantes*, and in black humor with the *pièces grinçantes*.

The collection of *pièces brillantes*, brilliant connoting brio, sophistication, and polish, includes *L'Invitation au Château* (1947), *Colombe* (1951), *La Répétition ou l'amour puni* (1950), and *Cécile ou l'école des pères* (1954).

L'Invitation au château (English translation, *Ring Round the Moon*) attests to one aspect of Anouilh's virtuosity which could easily sustain the discussion of an entire article. In this play, he accomplishes the feat of lending plausibility to the exits and entrances of identical twins played by the same actor. As a result of this achievement, he succeeds in so evenly distributing the action among the various characters that most of them spend an equal time on stage. The over-all result is that each character's situation is equally important and one cannot guess the outcome of the action. Here, the ending is a happy one, achieved by Anouilh when he combines the themes previously exploited in the *pièces noires*, so that money and love can exist side by side in harmony. A delight for stage directors, *Ring Round the Moon* is the Anouilh work most performed throughout the world in drama schools and amateur theatres.

To further exercise his theatrical boldness, Anouilh turned to the eighteenth-century French dramatist Marivaux, whose originality in plot construction and minute analysis of budding love is such that hardly any playwright has dared to imitate him. In *La Répétition ou l'amour puni* (English translation, *The Rehearsal*), Anouilh superimposes the technique of the play-within-a-play, as seen in Pirandello, on the framework of Marivaux's love comedy *La Double Inconstance*. He makes the blasé aristocrat and the delicate young teacher who are falling in love rehearse scenes of the Marivaux play, so that it is Marivaux's dialogue which serves to explain their feelings. At the same time, he weaves his own version of *La Double Inconstance* into the original one in order to establish a striking contrast betwen the cruel monsters of cynicism who make their appearance in the *pièces brillantes* and the valiant, innocent young girls found in both his and Marivaux's works who are also symbols of idealistic love. The play was so unanimously acclaimed in France that it was published in the *Classiques Larousse* collection as an example of a dazzling replica of Marivaux's comedy which at the same time captured the flavor of the twentieth-century theatre.

To top it all, Anouilh tried his hand at a faithful pastiche of another psychological comedy of Marivaux's in *Cécile ou l'école des pères* (Cécile; or, The School for Fathers). Called a jewel, this play was performed for the first time at the wedding of Anouilh's eldest daughter, Catherine. It deals with the relationship of a gracious father, as Anouilh is reputed to be, and his young daughter when she falls in love. As in previous *pièces brillantes*, here Anouilh is concerned with mastering yet another aspect of the French style. The play effortlessly recreates the accents of the subtle manners and speech of the French classical era.

[30]

It is doubtful that these last two works would be enjoyed by a public outside of France, for their charm originates in the very special tradition of the French theatre in the seventeenth and eighteenth centuries, which even a Frenchman must have studied to appreciate fully.

The key to the cycle of *pièces grinçantes* lies in the scene in *La Valse des Toréadors* during which General Saint-Pé becomes desperate at the thought that life is not at all what he had believed it to be. Perplexed, he turns to the doctor and asks him the meaning of all he has read in books, the grandiose loves, the prodigious revelations, the tender young girls who love men forever, the joy one feels at having at one's side a little "brother in arms" who changes into a lovable woman at night. The doctor answers calmly that these things represent the dreams of authors who must have been poor devils just like the general, and they both agree that such authors should be prevented from spreading false notions of this kind. The fabrications enumerated by the general are obvious references to Anouilh's themes in the *pièces noires*. Anouilh suddenly seems to be turning his back on the idealism expressed in his earlier work.

In the *pièces grinçantes* he no longer divides the world between idealists and realists, but fills it with ludicrous puppets and cynical hypocrites. He once praised Molière for having written the blackest form of theatre in a manner which made men laugh at their own misery and hideousness. As the use of the term "grinçantes" shows, Anouilh intends to do something similar in this new collection of plays. The word "grinçantes" implies, first, the interrupted motion of something which hits a snag. As such it can be applied to laughter interrupted by the awareness that one should probably cry. Secondly, it refers to the unpleasant sound of something which crushes or grinds, thus recalling the sound of things one does not really want to hear. It follows, then, that the laugh Anouilh wishes to extract must be brought about by a special brand of black humor. It is no surprise, therefore, that he introduces his first anti-hero, General Saint-Pé, in the first two *pièces grinçantes*, *Ardèle* and *La Valse des Toréadors*. As the first part of the general's name implies, he may wear the halo of the martyr, but as the second part ironically indicates, he will emerge from the plays as unwonted as a putrid bubble of human gas.

Although in *Ardèle* (1948) the action does not directly affect the general, it revolves around him. He starts out by leading a sort of burlesque ballet of people pursuing their personal images of love. What they call love turns out to be an amalgam of infantile sexuality, pathological fixation, and insolent mimicry. For a time he thinks he is conducting a family council, gathered to decide the fate of an aunt who is a hunchback and who is in love with another hunchback; in reality, he is accepting with a disturbing complacency the monstrous pronouncements of caricatures who indulge in a ludicrous masquerade of love. Unfortunately, he is too flighty to recognize the cannibalism hidden in their decision that hunchbacks have no right to love, and he chatters away unaware of the urgency of the situation he has created. But Anouilh soon destroys the mood of light banter with a brutal cascade of bullets. The shock of the incident reminds everyone that human souls are at stake, but it is too late. The poor hunchbacks have been left only one escape, suicide. Not one person has really cared about them. The voice of the young man who encouraged his aunt Ardèle to love, despite her relatives' advice, has gone unheard. Only the cackle of the caricatures Anouilh has painted here still rings in our ears. He evidently wants to convince us that idealism is pitifully destined to be drowned in the empty gibberish of the wicked and the futile. The general is totally inadequate to meet the responsibility he assumes when he locks up his sister, so he lets the hypocrites decide her fate. Thus he is just as guilty as they are of the ugly act which causes the death of the two innocents. And ugly acts have a way of propagating, as Anouilh points out in his last scene: The young children of the household are pretending to "be in love," so they imitate what they have seen their elders do, they fight like cats and dogs; with this sort of conception of love, we can envision that some day they will also decide on someone's right to love. Somehow the scene is so ludicrous that we smile, but from embarrassment, at the mere sight of such illogical behavior among men. Our smile is "grinçant," it cannot last long, for we realize there is a serious lesson hidden in that spectacle.

La Valse des Toréadors (1951; English translation, *The Waltz of the Toreadors*) sketches another episode in the life of General Saint-Pé. As it happens, he does not handle his own affairs any better than those of others. He continues to wait for someone or something, for "the right circumstances" to decide what he must do, for he is confused by the contradictions between what he is told and what he vaguely discovers to be true. But no one shows him the way. He is like Estragon and Vladimir waiting for Godot. He has not understood that man must jump at the slightest opportunity for fulfillment. Since life is a "ball that lasts only one night," he should dance as much as he can "before the colored lights go off." The moral of the play recalls the "Gather ye rosebuds while ye may" theme. But the general may have missed his chance out of fidelity to his wife; the moral may then be, as the doctor tells him, not to try to know "one's enemy, especially if it is a woman." The doctor implies that the general should not have postponed his happiness out of pity for his wife when he fell in love with Ghislaine, for, women being unpredictable, his sacrifice may prove to have been wasted. Although Anouilh exaggerates the play's cynicism for all its shock value, in reality he is asking whether it is worth while for the individual to cast aside his own happiness out of consideration for others who are themselves selfish. As we know, the general did not run away with Ghislaine the night he met her at the Saumure ball because he thought that his wife was deeply in love with him. Seventeen years later, while he still foolishly cherishes Ghislaine, his wife reveals to him that on that very night she left the ball and slept with a young officer. For having compromised and thought of others first, before reaching for his own happiness, General Saint-Pé ends up as a downtrodden buffoon, who wears a shiny uniform as if he were ready for a gala, but who has to find a pitiful solace in his kitchenmaid's skirts. Anouilh has provided the forbidding answer to his own question: at this point in his plays, ethics have disappeared into the realm of dreams.

There is no obvious tie between *Ardèle* and *La Valse des Toréadors*, other than the reappearance of General Saint-Pé. He emerges from both plays as an especially well-defined anti-hero who deserves close scrutiny. He represents especially the confused modern individual desperately trying to keep from drowning in the maze of contradictory forces which rule the world. He is made dizzy by the sweep of changing values in modern society, so he waits for a miraculous inspiration to move him in one direction or another. Since none materializes, he freezes into inaction. Face to face with evil, he does not recognize it or does not dare to acknowledge it. He struggles to find an ethic, although he is fallible enough to expect it to be easy to follow. A little cowardly, incredibly patient, he has been put on earth to be a victim, not a victor. He survives by sinking into sexual gratification, and by wearing a uniform which becomes his crutch. When he has the uniform on, others think that he is strong and brave. He knows that deep inside he is a lonely, frightened man, but appearances are good enough for him. He is Anouilh's image of today's man.

Ornifle, in the play *Ornifle ou le courant d'air* (1955; Ornifle; or, The Draft), is not a frightened man. He discovers, as does General Saint-Pé, that there can be no happy medium between honor and happiness. So he opts for happiness and then proceeds to laugh his way through life, often at the expense of those who are foolish enough to be gullible. Why should man, who does not ask to be born, spend his life surpassing himself? Society proves that any sort of self-denial is futile. Those who practice it are shy weaklings who deserve being used, or people who are possessed by an indecent brand of wickedness because they hide behind a mask of morality. So Ornifle will live for pleasure only.

This play succeeds in offering an interesting modern version of Molière's *Don Juan*. But Anouilh's motives when he created it were less innocent than Molière's. Whereas the action remains forbidding in both plays, Anouilh lends a more airy, flippant tone to his hero so as better to allow him to flaunt his views. Furthermore, when Ornifle collapses of a heart attack as he is about to engage in the betrayal of another weakling, the suddenness of his death does not imply punishment as it does in the Molière play, for Anouilh does not show that his death is inflicted by a mystic supernatural power stronger than he, as is the case with Don Juan. In this instance, Ornifle falls dead as if struck by lightning; thus Anouilh bestows on him an almost painless death, such as we think only innocent creatures deserve. Anouilh is saying that Ornifle was an innocent creature, for he did not hide his wickedness.

The play *Ornifle* represented a first shot at a specific target, since Anouilh, who usually alternates writing at least two different types of plays, doggedly pursued his course, and the following year, with *Pauvre Bitos ou le dîner de têtes* (English translation, *Poor Bitos*), published what appears to be the sequel to *Ornifle*.

In truth, the political events that provoked his anger co-incided with the point of development reached in his work that led him to write satires. In the early days of his voca-tion he had defended idealism in play after play. Then, as years passed and he looked more closely at the world, he dis-covered after World War II that more often than not idealism was a subterfuge used to cover the proverbial multitude of sins. He laughed in disenchantment at what might have been considered his naïveté. He was not certain whether it might not be that the world had changed so much that purity could no longer survive in it, so he seemed to ask those who had believed his beautiful images of purity not to take him too seriously. At times, it appeared that those who were pure enough to believe in tales of idealism were victimized either by life or by other men. Anouilh already knew the harsh rules of life; he now started to look at those who exploit men and he distinguished two kinds of opportunists: the Don Juan type, who openly join the forces of evil but who can be recognized, and the more dangerous variety, who wrap up their wickedness in all sorts of beautiful trappings. In *Pauvre Bitos*, the latter are the ones he pursues, while in *Ornifle* he shows how harmless openly wicked individuals actually may be.

After the Liberation of France, a political purge took place. The entire episode was odious, for it was based on finger-pointing and summary accusations, and sometimes it led to the executions of those who appeared to have "collaborated" with the Germans. Naturally, there were a number of unjust con-demnations and many people were revolted by the situation. Against this background Anouilh, who was already tormented by various forms of rampant hypocrisy and who had never wanted to judge men, wrote his first brilliant satire, *Pauvre Bitos*.

As might be expected, the play's strong impact derives from Anouilh's daring frankness and the clever device he chooses to denounce the true character of the *Epuration* (the Purge). By allowing the participants in the debate between Bitos and his tormentors to wear the headdress of French Revolutionary leaders, he makes them express their motives more forcefully, for they can act safely behind what amounts to a mask. Since Anouilh wants to show the French their unfortunate tendency to repeat mistakes, the parallelism with the Terror initiated by Robespierre during the Revolution serves to concretize and reinforce his theory.

The indictment is a very severe one, for Anouilh lashes out not only at Bitos, the righteous self-appointed "defender of the people," but also at his tormentors. Bitos, the spokesman for those who hunted the "collaborators," turns out to be a little narrow-minded man for whom education is a dangerous thing. He retains only the cold theory of education, and resents those who teach him anything and those who exert any authority over him. He is a demagogue who actually hates men and who has been biding his time until he could revenge himself upon all those who have shown more talent, more wealth, or more graciousness than he has. Because he suffered, he has to make others suffer by submitting them to rigid rules which he can justify only in abstract terms. Most scathing of all is the fact that he will come to terms with those whose ideas he despises in order to serve his own personal needs. The provocation of Bitos' obnoxious behavior shows Anouilh's irresistible urge to stylize the humiliating image of a man "caught with his pants down," hence the scene when Bitos splits his pants and has to bend over to have them sewed up again while still wearing them.

More repugnant than Bitos himself is the fact that such creatures have been used from time to time in France by government leaders who did not want to do the dirty work themselves but found a way to be accommodating to those who did. One of the characters, Brassac, points this out when he says that in France one can always find a general to sign a decree, and then add a retroactive clause if need be. The satire reaches its height when Anouilh turns the table on the tormentors of Bitos. They are rich bourgeois or aristocrats who think they belong to an elite which can sit in Olympian fashion and laugh at those who at least try to perform some social service; they do not possess courage enough to roll up their sleeves and serve their country also. As Deschamps, the only moderate character in the play besides Victoire, gently reminds them, their motives are no more admirable than those of Bitos, for all they do is take from society and never give in return if they can help it.

Strangely enough, many critics reacted to *Pauvre Bitos* by lamenting that Anouilh was a man who hated humanity. But the play is precisely an indictment addressed to those who treat humanity with cold, mechanized methods instead of indulgence, compassion, and love. Anouilh enjoins those who see man as an abstraction to open their eyes and see that men are made of flesh and blood.

When asked in August, 1969, what his favorite play was, Anouilh replied that it was *Pauvre Bitos:* first, because he had created a new character, which is always a "rosy" event in his life, and second, because he had dared to tell the French, at a time when it was unthinkable to do so, the things they needed to hear. What must be added is that satire is his natural medium of expression. The sweep of the discussion in *Pauvre Bitos* attests to that; so does the fact that in this form of drama his targets have no way of escaping his unrelenting scrutiny. Since he has the eye of Strindberg, the tongue of Shaw, and the aspirations of Molière, it has been hard for him not to choose exclusively to mock men for their weaknesses. There are signs that he may have come to acknowledge his talents in that field, for his widely acclaimed recent plays, *Cher Antoine* and *Les Poissons rouges*, are primarily satires.

Anouilh's propensity for lampooning does not mean that he necessarily looks for objects to blame. If possible, he would just as soon encounter moral beauty of the quality seen in *L'Alouette* (1952; English translation, *The Lark*) or *Becket ou l'honneur de Dieu* (1959; English translation, *Becket*). These two *pièces costumées* are, to date, his only serious yet optimistic plays. (The third *pièce costumée* is *La Foire d'empoigne* [1962].)

L'Alouette retells the martyrdom of Joan of Arc. In the Anouilh play, however, "The Lark," as he calls Joan of Arc, remains in full control of her trial except in one instance of weakness, from which she quickly recovers. As for Becket, the Archbishop of Canterbury, he forces Henry Plantagenet to reckon with the honor of the Church of England and the Saxons. Thus, as is expected of martyrs, both Joan and Becket emerge triumphant in death.

It would seem that at last, in these two plays, Anouilh found the pure idealism he had searched for in his earlier plays. By contrast with the heroes of the *pièces noires*, the heroine and hero of *L'Alouette* and *Becket*, respectively, give their lives for a cause which goes far beyond the self. They refuse the ways of materialism for definite reasons instead of ambiguous ones, as was the case with Gaston, Thérèse, and Antigone. Jeanne dies to protect the truth and to preserve the honor of the saints whose voices she heard. Becket accepts his own assassination in order to defend the honor of the Church of England, which he undertook to serve.

At the same time, these champions of idealism remain human and accessible instead of becoming alienated from humanity, as did the protagonists of the *pièces noires*. Jeanne continues to sympathize with her soldiers and never answers her tormentors angrily. Becket never looks down on the King or speaks scornfully of anyone. As a matter of fact, the validity and the beauty of both plays emanate from the delicate balance which Anouilh establishes in the psychology of all the characters. He goes to great lengths to avoid opposing abstract "types" to his protagonists. In *L'Alouette*, although both Cauchon and Warwick represent the opposition of materialism to Jeanne's spiritualism, Cauchon conveys the devious thirst for power hidden in some prelates, while Warwick displays the callousness of political expediency. In *Becket*, the King is a far more defined individual than Créon in *Antigone*. He is coarse, but he admires and understands the value of Becket's subtlety. His ruthlessness does not preclude his continued love for his protégé; he lucidly plans the defeat of Becket, but gallantly applauds him when he escapes the traps set for him. The King is a sympathetic mixture of roughness and tenderness.

As a result of this careful characterization, we feel that, although the characters do not share the ideals of their opponents, they still belong to the same "race." There is no need for two groups, one, the elected, and the other the damned, as there was in the *pièces noires*. The protagonists' plight in the *pièces costumées* seems the more pathetic, since there should be a way for at least the men of the same group to live in harmony.

Although the two plays are similar so far as meaning is concerned, any resemblance stops there. Each one does far more than conform to the patterned discussion of idealism which Anouilh started in his early plays. *Becket* unfurls the gripping history of a friendship which was meant to bring each partner lifelong comfort; it is the story of a mutual affection which lasts even through adversity. *L'Alouette* illustrates

Anouilh's image of the lark that still sings in the sky while being shot at. It depicts the combination of strength and vulnerability that characterizes mankind. It is proof of the moral indestructibility of the man or the woman who is truly good.

Both excellent plays in which no aspect of dramatization has been neglected, *L'Alouette* and *Becket* had long runs on Broadway. The dialogue in the case of each is a masterpiece of nuances. In *Becket* the strong, earthy language of the King and the barons is played against the measured, restrained language which Becket uses to seek understanding. In *L'Alouette*, Jeanne uses a language which seems rudimentary, but which translates her acute common sense in such a way that what she says becomes irrefutable. At the same time, Cauchon uses expressions filled with double meaning, while the short exclamations of the *promoteur* betray his lewdness in a hilarious manner. The pageantry one expects in a historical play is smoothly fitted into the plot so that one has the impression of witnessing an authentic yet modernized version of the story. Anouilh pushes the boldness of staging to the point of representing people on horseback, in both plays. Finally, to stress the victory of the protagonists and to allow the spectator the satisfaction of a happy ending, he uses the flashback in various ways so that the last scene is one of triumph. The spectator leaves the theatre not with the image of Jeanne being burned but with the sight of her radiant as she watches the consecration of the King of France. *Becket* ends not with the assassination of the Archbishop but, as it had started, with the flogging of the repentant King in the church. Here, the body of the play constitutes the flashback.

The *pièces costumées* constitute the last volume of grouped plays published to date. Following this series, Anouilh concentrated on individual plays, including *La Grotte* (English translation, *The Cavern*), edited in book form in 1961. A clever mystery play of Pirandellian inspiration, supposedly written under the spectator's eyes, it introduces a long-awaited character in Anouilh's theatre, "the author," who becomes Antoine de Saint-Flour in *Cher Antoine ou l'amour raté* and in *Les Poissons rouges*.

In 1962, a one-act "concert play," *L'Orchestre* (The Orchestra), appeared in *L'Avant-Scène*, a literary journal. The same year Anouilh unknowingly took a major step in his development when he re-created *Victor ou les enfants au pouvoir* (Victor; or, The Children in Power), written by a long-time friend, the late Roger Vitrac; in this surrealistic play he found a technique which answered his own yearning to stylize the flow of human consciousness for the theatre. Directed for the first time in 1928 by Antonin Artaud at the Théâtre Alfred Jarry, this work had been very poorly received by public and critics alike. When Anouilh saw *Victor* produced by the Michel de Ré Company in 1947, he was so extraordinarily impressed by it that, as he has admitted, he slightly plagiarized it in *Ardèle*. His own production of *Victor* fifteen years later won wide acclaim. A subtly poetic "bourgeois drama," this play deals with Anouilh's favorite topic, the family circle; the plot focuses on the cruel fate of a child who suddenly realizes the true aspect of the adult world and who accepts, along with this knowledge, his symbolic death. Anouilh was ready to investigate this particular subject; but more important than its thematic value, *Victor* offered him an example of dialogue which follows the capricious meanderings of the consciousness of some of the characters.

Le boulanger, la boulangère et le petit mitron (The Baker, His Wife, and His Little Apprentice), the first play written by Anouilh in the six years following his production of *Victor*, shows the repercussions of his faithful efforts to vindicate Vitrac. In it, a child becomes the central character and the play develops according to all the swirls and eddies of the stream of consciousness.

As far as children are concerned, Anouilh became preoccupied with their condition in the so-called family bosom quite early in his vocation with *Humulus le muet* and *Le Voyageur sans bagage*. Later, he concentrated his attentions on adults. But after his exposure to *Victor*, he again gave a larger share of the limelight to children, reserving special treatment for the small boy Toto. In *Ardèle*, Toto is first encountered as the child whose presence is overlooked by the family plunged into its petty problems. With Anouilh's delighted approval, he unconsciously gets even with his family by mimicking its grotesque behavior at the most crucial moment. In *L'Hurluberlu* (English translation, *The Fighting Cock*), Toto becomes an incarnation of General Saint-Pé's childhood. When the general encourages him to eat a dose of magic "mininistafia," he is addressing not only his little boy but also the alter ego of his own youth, the vestiges of which are still visible in himself. In *Les Poissons rouges* Toto attains a more complex status. He brings consolation to his father, the playwright Antoine de Saint-Flour, and to the extent that Anouilh can be identified with Antoine de Saint-Flour, one wonders how much of Toto is still a part of Anouilh.

In *Le boulanger, la boulangère et le petit mitron*, Toto represents all children. Writing this tragicomic bedroom farce in the aftermath of the euphemistically titled "May events" (the student revolt in Paris of May, 1968), Anouilh doggedly insists on showing the origins of the social troubles involving young people: in his view, children are abandoned and pitifully lost in the average family, where "Papa" takes refuge from his wife and his boss in dreams of power and feminine conquests, while "Maman" either flies away into dreams of passionate love or complains because she is not living in the grand style she feels she deserves. If the wife in this play is to be believed, had she married one of the glamorous suitors who lined up at her door before she condescended to marry her husband, she would have lived like a queen.

In a preface written in defense of young people, Anouilh points out that, although children are neglected within their families, they must be psychoanalyzed and submitted to bewildering tests when they dare to revolt and ask for their rights in a society hopelessly oblivious of their existence and needs and primarily concerned with the rights of adults. The French public did not take too kindly to Anouilh's position and in a short while refrained from seeing the play, although it was hailed as a triumphant sort of comeback on Anouilh's part.

The value of *Le boulanger, la boulangère et le petit mitron* lies especially in its surrealistic structure. Anouilh would object to the use of the term "surrealistic," for when he commented on Vitrac's *Victor* he purposely avoided it; he considers surrealism in the theatre an evolution of the desire to represent the flow of consciousness, which, as he declared in an interview, was started by Aeschylus and was continued by Corneille, Shakespeare, and Pirandello. It is not surprising that Anouilh has tried his hand at surrealism, for he has steadily torn down the barriers betwen illusion and reality. In this play, the dialogue exchanged on a conscious level by the protagonists matters little as compared to the dialogue they use when they engage in their daydreaming, for it is then that their motives and their foolishness come to the fore, providing an explanation of their unreasonable behavior. Toto's dilemma also draws its emphasis from the impeccably timed intrusions of his own daydreams into his parents' flight into fantasy. Peopled with storybook Indians and poetic historical figures, such as Louis XVI, Marie Antoinette, and their children facing danger as a family, Toto's dreams help us to measure the void in which he grows up. Though he should find warmth in the family nest, he must instead seek solace from his parents' bewildering quarrels in his books. And while he needs guidance and encouragement in the arduous steps of getting an education, he must study his history lesson in utter loneliness, drawing conclusions as best he can.

Modern society has ceased to produce truly mature adults and the children's problems stem from that fact, says Anouilh. It is significant that in his portrayal of the infantilism of present-day adults, some of the father's flights into illusion originate in the little boy's questions about American Indians (who still belong to the realm of fiction for the French). The father thus proves he stands just a step removed from the world of make-believe that his child lives in.

Begun as a bedroom farce, the play becomes a voyage into the inextricable mixture of reality and dream in which the characters are immersed, and it ends with Toto's nightmare about his parents getting killed by Indians. Such an end is particularly effective, for within the play it serves to explain how Toto finds release from the mental torture caused by his parents' incessant arguments; outside of the play it satisfies somewhat the spectator's need to see the parents punished for their incorrigible thoughtlessness. Nevertheless, when the Lieutenant kindly takes Toto under his protection and asks forgiveness for the parents, who have simply behaved like fallible human beings, the play closes on a compassionate note.

It was inevitable that Anouilh, indefatigable observer of men, would reach a point where he could not remain impassive at the sight of the excesses they commit, and would create a sort of spokesman. He did so in *Cher Antoine ou l'amour raté* (Dear Antoine; or, Lost Love), his first play of the 1969–70 season, where he introduced the playwright Antoine de Saint-Flour. After obtaining rave reviews for this play, Anouilh daringly presented a second play that season, *Les Poissons rouges ou mon père ce Héros* (The Goldfish; or, My Father, That Hero), where the same protagonist, seen at an earlier time, takes stock of himself. As he searches his past and present, he discovers that, whereas he has tried to be a compassionate, fairly honorable human being, he is held responsible for every possible ill by the people around him. At home, his wife nags him, his mother-in-law remains unconcerned at his being abused, his fifteen-year-old daughter declares she became pregnant out of wedlock so she could leave home. In the outside world, a childhood friend, who is a worker's son and whom he treats with unusual forbearance, insults him, morning, noon, and night, as if he had caused all the social ills the proletariat suffers from. Even his mistress is afflicted with suicidal obsessions and complicates his life no end. Plagued by all this, Antoine comes to feel at times that he should walk like a hunchback or even limp, in order to placate hunchbacks like his doctor (a frustrated literary critic) who chastises him for being healthy.

Permeated with the good-natured reactions of Antoine, opposed to the sourness and self-righteousness of others, the play greatly amuses by its wealth of impish repartee. In the exchange lies many a truth about the privileged and the not-so-privileged of our society. "Refreshing" is the epithet critics have used to qualify this comedy both *rose* and *noire*. Actually, Anouilh has never been anything else.

SELECTED BIBLIOGRAPHY

NOTE: *All the works of Jean Anouilh are published in French by La Table Ronde, Paris, unless otherwise indicated.*

Principal Works of Jean Anouilh

Pièces noires (L'Hermine, La Sauvage, Le Voyageur sans bagage, Eurydice). 1945.

Nouvelles pièces noires (Jézabel, Antigone, Roméo et Jeannette, Médée). 1947.

Pièces grinçantes (Ardèle ou la marguerite, La Valse des Toréadors, Ornifle ou le courant d'air, Pauvre Bitos ou le dîner de têtes). 1956.

Pièces roses (Humulus le muet, Le Bal des voleurs, Le Rendez-vous de Senlis, Léocadia). 1958.

Pièces brillantes (L'Invitation au château, Colombe, La Répétition ou l'amour puni, Cécile ou l'école des pères). 1960.

Pièces costumées (L'Alouette, Becket ou l'honneur de Dieu, La Foire d'empoigne). 1960.

La Petite Molière, in *L'Avant-Scène*, No. 210, December 15, 1959.

L'Hurluberlu ou le réactionnaire amoureux. 1959.

La Grotte. 1961.

L'Orchestre, in *L'Avant-Scène*, No. 276, November 15, 1962.

Le boulanger, la boulangère et le petit mitron. 1969.

Cher Antoine ou l'amour raté. 1969.

Les Poissons rouges ou mon père ce héros. 1970.

Translations of Jean Anouilh's Plays

Five Plays. 2 vols. New York, Hill and Wang, 1958–59.
> Vol. 1. Antigone, Eurydice, The Ermine, The Rehearsal (La Répétition), Romeo and Jeannette.
> Vol. 2. Restless Heart (La Sauvage), Time Remembered (Léocadia), Ardèle, Mademoiselle Colombe, The Lark (L'Alouette).

Ring Round the Moon (L'Invitation au château). Tr. Christopher Fry, with a preface by Peter Brook. New York, Oxford University Press, 1950.

Thieves' Carnival (Le Bal des voleurs). Tr. Lucienne Hill. London, Methuen, 1952.

The Waltz of the Toreadors. Tr. Lucienne Hill. New York, Samuel French, 1958.

Traveller without Luggage (Le voyageur sans bagage). Tr. John Whiting. London, Methuen, 1959.

Becket; or The Honor of God. Tr. Lucienne Hill. New York, Coward-McCann, 1960.

The Fighting Cock (L'Hurluberlu). Adapted by Lucienne Hill. New York, Coward-McCann, 1960.

Poor Bitos. Tr. Lucienne Hill. New York, Coward-McCann, 1964.

The Cavern (La Grotte). Tr. Lucienne Hill. New York, Hill and Wang, 1966.

Critical Works and Commentary

NOTE: *An extensive bibliography of critical books and articles on Jean Anouilh's work through 1968 may be found in* French VII Bibliography (*New York, The French Institute*).

de Luppé, Robert. Jean Anouilh, suivi des fragments de la pièce de J. Anouilh: *Oreste*. Paris, Ed. Universitaires, 1959.

Didier, Jean. Jean Anouilh. Liège, La Sixaine, 1946.

Gignoux, Hubert. Jean Anouilh. Paris, Ed. du Temps présent, 1946.

Lassalle, Jean-Pierre. Jean Anouilh ou la vaine révolte. Rodez, Ed. Subervie, 1958.

Marcel, G. L'Heure théâtrale. Paris, Plon, 1959.

Marsh, E. O. Jean Anouilh, Poet of Pierrot and Pantaloon. London, W. H. Allen, 1953.

Pronko, L. C. The World of Jean Anouilh. Berkeley and Los Angeles, University of California Press, 1961.

Interviews

Ambrière, Francis. "Le secret de Jean Anouilh," *Les Annales*, XV (January, 1952), 45.

Archer, Marguerite. Paris, August 25, 1962; Arcachon, August 3, 1969. Also present at this second interview was Roland Piétri, Amouilh's long-time co-stage director.

Delavèze, Jean. "Pour la première fois Jean Anouilh parle. . . ," *Les Nouvelles Littéraires*, February 5, 1959, pp. 1, 9.

Farrell, Isolde. "Anouilh Returns," *New York Times*, January 3, 1954, Sec. 2, p. x3.